MUHAMMAD ALI

The Greatest

by Joanne Mattern

Content Consultant
Nanci R. Vargus, Ed.D.
Professor Emeritus, University of Indianapolis

Reading Consultant
Jeanne M. Clidas, Ph.D.
Reading Specialist

Children's Press®
An Imprint of Scholastic Inc.

Library of Congress Cataloging-in-Publication Data
Names: Mattern, Joanne, 1963- author.
Title: Muhammad Ali: the greatest / by Joanne Mattern.
Description: New York, NY : Children's Press, [2017] | Series: Rookie biographies | Includes index.
Identifiers: LCCN 2016030343 | ISBN 9780531221174 (library binding) |
ISBN 9780531224472 (pbk.)
Subjects: LCSH: Ali, Muhammad, 1942-2016—Juvenile literature. | Boxers (Sports)—United States—
Biography—Juvenile literature.
Classification: LCC GV1132.A4 M38 2017 | DDC 796.83092 [B]—dc23
LC record available at https://lccn.loc.gov/2016030343

Produced by Spooky Cheetah Press
Design by Judith Christ-Lafond
Poem by Jodie Shepherd

© 2017 by Scholastic Inc.

Printed in China 62

SCHOLASTIC, CHILDREN'S PRESS, ROOKIE BIOGRAPHIES™, and associated logos are trademarks and/or registered trademarks of Scholastic Inc.

1 2 3 4 5 6 7 8 9 10 R 26 25 24 23 22 21 20 19 18 17

Photographs ©: cover main: The Stanley Weston Archive/Getty Images; cover background, back cover background: blueringmedia/iStockphoto; 3: allanswart/Thinkstock; 4-5: Harry Benson/Getty Images; 6: Private Collection/Christie's Images/Bridgeman Art Library; 8: Popperfoto/Getty Images; 10: AP Images; 11: Central Press/Getty Images; 12: AP Images; 15: AP Images; 16: Underwood Archives/Getty Images; 18-19: AP Images; 20: AP Images; 23: Marty Lederhandler/AP Images; 24: Paula Bronstein/Getty Images; 26: Scott Halleran/Getty Images; 27: Michael Cooper/Getty Images; 29: Ty Wright/Getty Images; 30: wabeno/Thinkstock; 31 center top: Abel Tumik/Shutterstock, Inc.; 31 bottom: Central Press/Getty Images; 31 center bottom: AP Images; 31 top: AP Images; 32: Arsen Stakhiv/iStockphoto.

Maps by Mapping Specialists

TABLE OF CONTENTS

Ali worked hard to become a great boxer.

4

Meet Muhammad Ali

Boxer Muhammad Ali (muh-HAH-med ah-LEE) was one of the most famous fighters of all time. He was not only a **champion** athlete. He was a hero to people all over the world.

Muhammad Ali was born on January 17, 1942, in Louisville, Kentucky. His birth name was Cassius Clay. His father was a sign painter. His mother cooked and cleaned for other families. He had a younger brother named Rudy.

FAST FACT!

Cassius and Rudy loved to play rough. Friends called them "the Wrecking Crew."

Rudy

Cassius

CANADA

UNITED STATES

KENTUCKY

Louisville

MEXICO

Area enlarged

MAP KEY

● City where Muhammad Ali was born

When Cassius was 12 years old, someone stole his brand-new bike. A policeman named Joe Martin came to find out what happened. Cassius told Martin that he wanted to beat up the person who stole his bike. Martin had a better idea. He suggested Cassius join his boxing class.

Cassius was just a kid when he started boxing.

Clay trained hard. When he was just 17, he won a big championship called the Golden Gloves. The next year, in 1960, Clay was part of the United States Olympic Team. He won every fight and earned a gold medal.

Olympic gold medal, front and back

FAST FACT!

By the time he was 18, Clay had won 100 out of 108 fights!

LISTON

31	**AGE**	23
212	**WEIGHT**	210
	HEIGHT	
6 ft. 1 in.		6 ft. 3 in.
	REACH	
84 in.		79 in.
	CHEST NORMAL	
44 in.		43 in
	CHEST EXPANDED	
46 ½ in.		45 in.
	WAIST	
33 in.		34 in.
	FOREARM	
14 ½ in.		13 ½ in.
	FIST	
15 ½ in.		13 in.
	NECK	
17 ½ in.		17 ¾ in.
	BICEPS	
17 ½ in.		16 in.

After the Olympics, Clay became a professional boxer. He was big and strong, but he did not win on strength alone. Clay had a different style from other boxers.

He danced around the ring. He was very fast. He made his **opponents** tired. Then he hit them—hard. In 1964, Clay beat Sonny Liston to become the **heavyweight** champion of the world.

Triumph and Trouble

For years, African Americans had faced unfair treatment simply because of the color of their skin. During the 1960s, they were fighting for equal rights.

Clay was part of that fight, called the Civil Rights Movement. He also joined a group called the Nation of Islam. He changed his name to Muhammad Ali.

Ali with civil rights leader
Martin Luther King Jr. (left)

15

Ali was never shy about sharing his thoughts!

America was also involved in a war in Vietnam. Ali refused to fight in the war. Many people were angry. Ali's championship was taken away. At 25 years old, Ali was at the height of his career. But he was not allowed to box anymore. Ali did not care. He stood up for what he believed in.

FAST FACT!

Ali could not box, but he could still talk! He made hundreds of speeches about civil rights.

Return of a Champion

In the early 1970s, Ali was allowed to box again. In 1974, he traveled to Africa to fight a boxer named George Foreman. The match was called "the Rumble in the Jungle." Ali won. Once again, he was the heavyweight champion of the world.

Ali knocked Foreman out in round 8 of the match.

Ali holds the trophy from his win over Frazier.

In 1975, Ali fought a powerful boxer named Joe Frazier. The two men met in Manila in the Philippines. The fight was called "the Thrilla in Manila." Ali and Frazier fought very hard. Both men were hurt and tired. But Ali won the fight.

FAST FACT!

Ali often made up rhymes about himself. One of the most famous was, "Float like a butterfly, sting like a bee. The hands can't hit what the eyes can't see."

New Challenges

Ali lost the heavyweight title to Leon Spinks in 1978.
A few months later, he won it back. But Ali was slowing down. He lost several fights. He was almost 40 years old. That is old for a boxer!
Ali finally retired in 1981.

FAST FACT!

Ali is the only boxer to win the heavyweight title three times.

Ali always made time for his fans.

Ali visits a girls' school in Afghanistan.

In 1984, Ali faced a new fight. He told the world he had Parkinson's disease. This disease affects the brain. It makes it hard to walk, move, or speak. Still, Ali kept busy helping others around the world. He helped children and people with **disabilities**. He also helped others who had Parkinson's disease.

In 1996, Ali received a great honor. He was asked to light the Olympic flame at the Summer Games in Atlanta, Georgia. After that, Ali was not seen much in public. Instead, he spent time with his nine children.

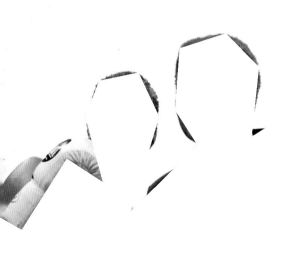

Ali's daughter Laila also became a boxer.

Ali poses with the Olympic torch.

On June 3, 2016, Muhammad Ali died. He was 74. People everywhere honored this man who was more than an athlete. Ali was true to his beliefs, and worked hard to be the greatest.

Timeline of Muhammad Ali's Life

1942	1960	1964
Born on January 17	Wins Olympic gold medal	Named heavyweight champion Changes name

Returns to boxing

Dies on June 3

1967 > **1970** > **1981** > **2016**

Banned from
boxing

Retires from boxing

A Poem About Muhammad Ali

Muhammad Ali was quick as a fox,
but he did far more than simply box.
He spoke out for justice and for civil rights,
and no one was better at winning fights.

You Can Be a Champion

Stand up for what you believe in. Do not let other people talk you out of your beliefs.

Be your best at whatever you choose to do.

Work hard to achieve success.

Glossary

champion (CHAM-pee-uhn): winner of a competition

disabilities (diss-uh-BIH-luh-teez): conditions that limit people's abilities to move, sense things, or perform activities

heavyweight (HEH-vee WATE): professional boxer weighing more than 175 pounds

opponents (uh-POH-nuhnts): people or teams you play or compete against in a contest

Index

Facts for Now

Visit this Scholastic Web site for more information on Muhammad Ali
and download the Teaching Guide for this series:
www.factsfornow.scholastic.com
Enter the keywords Muhammad Ali

About the Author

Joanne Mattern has written more than 250 books for children.
She especially likes writing biographies because she loves to learn about
real people and the things they do. Joanne also enjoys watching sports,
although she is not very good at playing them! She grew up in New York
State and still lives there with her husband, four children, and several pets.

7